Low Content Publishing

Amy Harrop

Low Content Publishing: How to Publish and Profit with No Writing Needed

By **Amy Harrop**

Printed in the United States of America

Copyright © 2020 Amy Harrop

Neither the author nor the publisher assumes any responsibility for the use or misuse of information contained in this book.

ISBN: 978-1545045763

Table of Contents

INTRODUCTION

One of the most exciting income opportunities of the past 10 years has been the rise of self-publishing.

Starting with eBooks, self-publishing has helped thousands of people make additional income and fulfill their dreams.

What if I told you that the opportunities for self-publishing are open to everyone...not just writers?

With today's technology, anyone can publish and profit.

How?

With low and no content books.

Now, anyone can use print-on-demand technology to publish consumable books that people love, all with very little upfront cost.

In this guide, I'll reveal:

- The amazing opportunities in low content publishing

- How you can get started with very little upfront cost

- The most popular niches and topics

And by implementing these strategies, you can stand out in a crowded marketplace and increase your publishing royalties and income.

1 WHAT ARE LOW AND NO CONTENT BOOKS?

Low and no content books refer to books that have little or repetitive content.

Believe it or not, these types of books are quite popular with customers, because they function as tools for a variety of processes, procedures, and events.

Blank books are ideal for:
- Journals
- Planners
- Event books
- Coloring books

There are massive opportunities for publishers with low or no content books.

What is great about these is that even though they have zero, little, or repetitive content they can easily be customized to fit a huge variety of niches and needs.

They fall into one of two broad categories: truly blank books or those with very repetitive content.

For example, look at a journal. You may get a few words here and there, but the book is largely blank so that you can fill it with your own writing.

There are also books with little content that are not truly blank, but certainly are not as complex as a novel, such as a coloring book or a planning book.

Aside from some formatting and pictures, all of these books are essentially blank.

While it may not seem like it, especially since so little work is involved, this is a thriving industry.

Why do you think bookstores are always putting out new blank books and why do you think that every year they rush to make new planners and journals?

Because, these books sell. Whether as something useful or just as an impulse buy, blank books can become indispensable to publishers, especially if they are made correctly.

Advantages

Some of the advantages of publishing these books include:

- Very low investment of time or money in terms of creating content.
- Ability to target a wide variety of demographics and niches.

- Versatility: can easily sell these types of books, both as a book and as a physical product.
- Ability to scale: you can easily repurpose your book into other niches and categories that are popular. In addition, you can create more books easily.

2 POPULAR TYPES OF BOOKS

These are the five most popular types of low content books:

- Journals
- Event Books
- Planners and Logs
- Coloring Books
- Recipe Books

Popularity

Let us now take a closer look at some commonalities of popular sellers in each category and what type of content they normally include:

Journals

The most consistent sellers in the blank book realm tend to be generic ones, such as truly blank journals and planners with minimal formatting.

These are books that are largely composed of lines and little else. They might have some witty sayings or one-liners here and there, but that is about it. While you can make a truly blank journal with nothing inside of it, there is content you can add to the journal to help increase sales and the connection to the audience.

Writing Journal

Another popular type of journal is one geared specifically toward writers. Yes, people can easily type or even speak their notes, but nothing beats the intimacy of writing your personal thoughts and feelings with a pen. These are usually general purpose books and essentially do not need any content.

However, you can write down a few lines here and there like, "How are you feeling today?" or "Don't worry, I'll keep it a secret." You can also include writing prompts that they can respond to via journaling. What you write can allow you to target certain ages, genders, and overall demographics, so be sure that you keep it within the right group.

Dream Journal

Everyone has dreams, and most of us want to remember them either because they are unique or because popular psychology teaches us that dreams are doorways to the mind. A dream journal gives someone a specific area to write their dreams, and you can even add some content here and there to target this market.

There are two ways of going about this, and there is nothing wrong with combining them:

First, you can write down little prompts here and there about reminding people to write their dreams as soon as they wake up like, "Dream or Nightmare? Tell me what you remember."

The second way is giving small tips for better recalling dreams or even having lucid dreams. For example, some experts say that you should slowly wear out your mind or focus on certain details to remind yourself that you are in a dream.

You can also include quotes about dreams to inspire them. Later in this report I will share a list of websites in which you can get quotes you can include in your book as content.

Prayer Journal

Prayer books are very simple, and many times you can just copy and paste content to put a book together. These are like general purpose journals, but the purpose is to remind people what or who they should pray for.

So, what content works best here?

You can write psalms, verses, or even obscure portions of whatever religious text you are taking from. These books can be targeted towards any religion, though Christianity is the most popular.

Diet Journal

Did you know that writing a food journal is one of the best and most scientifically proven ways to lose weight? Most people who are overweight have lost touch with what they eat. They forget about all the empty calories they are ingesting and the account of the amount of food they are taking in during the day.

Food journals have become much more popular. While digital versions do very well, especially calculating calories within seconds, many people still prefer to hand write in their food journal.

So, what can you add to these books?

Remind people to write down everything they have eaten. Also remind people to write some basic diet tips, like proper serving sizes (like how meat should be the size of your palm), or how vegetables are proven to keep you fuller and reduce weight.

You can also add some weight-loss motivational sayings in the margins to make people feel good about their personal journey.

Gratitude Journal

In many ways this is similar to the prayer book. Many people even consider it a religious duty to be grateful towards their chosen deity for what he or she has bestowed upon them. On the other hand, this can also be a general book to remind people to have gratitude for the things around them. The point of these books is that it gives people a space to write about the things they like, which in turn tend to make them feel better and focus on the good instead of the bad.

Aside from writing general things like, "What are you grateful for today?" or "What made your life better today?" you can also write motivational lines like how it is always better to look at the good. It is healthy to remember what you are grateful for and so on. Motivation and feeling good are the main things to hit with this market.

Planners and Logs

Actionable planners, which make the user feel like he or she has to do something, are quite popular right now. Those with detailed formatting tend to be the best as it allows the user to make full use of the planner. In fact, planners are often judged by how much space and how many areas people are given.

We all have things to do, but some of us either have too much to remember or others may easily forget tasks unless they are written down. In either case, planners are an essential element for busy people. These books typically do not have any text outside of a few words, so formatting takes the spotlight here.

Homework Planners

Homework planners are most typically made for high school and college students, but younger students may also use them. Some planners are very short. A specific planner can fit a whole week's worth of homework in two pages. This is done by having all the major classes (English, math, and etc.) with a few lines so that the user can write the assignment.

Others are much larger, which are typically for college students. They will be an area where the student can write the subject and assignment, another area for notes (such as for tests or things to study), and other areas for overall thoughts or plans.

Regardless of how it is done, it is best to list a few subjects and then allow the student to write other subjects as needed. How much space you give students is based largely on preference, demographic, and your particular formatting style.

Calendar Planners

These are considered the most generic planners because it basically just gives the person enough space to write his or her plans for a certain day. Many business people use these planners because they need to do certain things or be certain places on specific dates.

Some of these planners are fairly thin. This is done by providing large calendars in which there is only a little space to write. Others go day by day, devoting a page or two to each day. These sort of planners tend to be more popular because people want enough room to write all of their plans.

Event Books

We all have major events that happen to us, from weddings and birthdays to death and retirement. Everyone has major events that had happened to them, and some people want to remember as much as they can of the event through pictures, words, and so on. Blank event books give people a way to record their memories in a formatted space. Unlike journals, pictures are typically more important here, but it is also a good idea to add spaces so that people can write their feelings.

These books can be targeted to specific demographics, and swaying the book towards some demographic will typically improve sales. However, there is nothing wrong with making a book that people can completely customize to their needs.

Wedding, Pregnancy, Milestones & Special Events

These are hybrid books that are like journals, photo books, and planners all in one. There are spaces where people can place photos of a wedding, pregnancy, graduation, or other events. These sorts of planners also come with writing spaces where people can write their feelings. They are often guided, like "Top five names if it's a boy" or "What she made me do right before the wedding."

There are also typically planner sections, such as "30 days before birth" and "What we need done by (date)." Photos are normally the major highlight here, but the other sections are important as well, so be sure to add everything into these blank books.

Coloring Books

You might also be surprised to know that, aside from popular kids' characters, adult coloring books are quite popular. These books include intricate designs and patterns. You can make your own patterns for these books, and you can also make your own cast of characters for kids' coloring books (such as underwater characters).

This is quite a broad category, and you might be surprised to know that coloring books are not just for kids. However, let us start with younger readers:

If you are targeting young children, simple shapes and characters are probably the best. Slightly older kids will like themed books, like undersea adventures or sci-fi pictures.

There are also adult coloring books, believe it or not, and they are quite popular on Amazon. These books have complex designs, such as mandalas or abstract 3d spaces that people can color in to create intricate designs. If you are an artist, you can try your hand at making these types of books, but it is much easier to stick with the former and make simple designs for children.

Recipe Books

Everyone has those recipes that they love whether they are original creations, are found in magazines, or heard from other people. Regardless, people have recipes that they want to remember. While chefs can be targeted in this market, it is just as viable to make a book for anyone who likes to cook.

The most cohesive books have sections for ingredients, cooking methods, and other steps along with recipe time (for prep and cooking) and any other notes that the person may need to enter. These books are typically straightforward, and you may want to include a few pictures of food here and there, or just keep it simple.

3 NICHES AND CATEGORIES

While I have shared some of the broader categories for the low and no content books, keep in mind that you can niche these up quite a bit.

What I mean is you can narrow your demographics to appeal to specific interests.

For example, you could have a journal that features pets. So it could be a dog or cat themed journal with cute quotes and pictures of dogs or cats. You could even have a pet journal that is about a pet's milestones, similar to a baby book.

You could also have journals and logbooks that are geared toward specific hobbies.

For example, you could have one that logs sporting events, hunting, fishing, travel, and etc.

If there is a strong interest in a specific niche, chances are they would welcome a low or no content book that is themed toward their interests.

Categories

One of the most important aspects of understanding how to be successful with publishing low/no content books is picking the best categories for your books on Amazon.

Secret Categories

One reason why these books sell well is they can live in many different categories inside Amazon and not just books!

One of the 'secrets' of selling your book on Amazon is that you can sell many books, including these types of books, in non-book categories.

However, you will need to be set up as an Amazon seller which is completely different than selling through KDP. There are many benefits to selling this way, though.

Not only can you sell your books in other non-book categories, but you can also bulk print your books.

The best way to take advantage of this is to send your books directly to Amazon and sell them through their Prime Program.

4 PRINTING YOUR BOOK

Before we get into designing your book, it is important to take a look at where you can print your book and what are the specifications for printing your book. That way, you have an idea of what you will need to design your book.

There are three main places to consider for publishing. I am suggesting them because they offer a variety of options like:
- Print on Demand
- Bulk Printing
- Distribution Options

There are also other companies that offer bulk printing of notebooks and blank books like:

- http://spiralnotebooks.net

- https://www.jakprints.com/notebooks.html

- https://printpps.com/custom-spiral-notebooks/products/

- https://www.deluxe.com/products/promotional/journals-notebooks/

However, they do not offer any distribution or POD options.

Basically, I would suggest taking a 2-prong approach:

- Get extended distribution and sell your low/no content book as a book through one of these services.
- Order the book yourself in bulk from the service and also sell as a product on Amazon through their FBA program.

Printing Formats and Binding

You should review popular books in your niche and category and decide what size and format you want your book to be. I suggest keeping the interior in black and white, especially for your first book, in order to keep costs down.

Specialty Formats and Binding

For some type of specialty books, you may need to go beyond these templates and do some more research, such as for photo albums or specialty journals. You may want to stick to a simpler template or format for your first project.

File Type

If we are talking about the file type, you will then be surprised to know that nearly any file type that includes text or pictures will be accepted. It is best to go with PDF or .Epub formats. This ensures that you do not have to worry about sizing issues, fonts being changed (especially if you use uncommon ones), or other potential issues.

Templates

The best and easiest way to create a print ready PDF is to use a template. You will also need to make sure when you export content to PDF that it is print ready. This is something you can either do yourself or you can have a designer do for you.

I suggest using Amazon KDP as a resource, even if you do not do your printing through them.

You can get free Kindle Direct Publishing templates and Microsoft Word for a variety of print sizes here:

- https://kdp.amazon.com/en_US/help/topic/G201834230

- https://www.bookbaby.com/templates

- https://www.diggypod.com/how-to-publish-a-book/templates-and-margins/

- https://www.48hrbooks.com/free-book-templates

- http://www.diybookformats.com/mswordt emplates/

Simply pick the size that you want for your book, I would suggest looking at the most common sizes for the type of book you want to create.

You can then use that as your template. If you are working in Microsoft Word (more on programs later) or if you are working in another type of program you can mimic the page setup.

Some of the most common sizes for low/no content books are:

- 6x9 inches
- 8.5 x11 inches
- 9 x9 inches

For print ready PDF specifications, check out this Amazon KDP guide:

- https://kdp.amazon.com/en_US/help/topic /G201834230

KDP also offers cover templates. It can also assist you to use and adapt the templates to create your physical book cover:

- https://kdp.amazon.com/en_US/cover-templates

Here are three of the main POD providers, their distribution options, and their pros and cons.

Ingram Spark

https://www.ingramspark.com/

Ingram is one of the world's top book distributors.

It sells internationally to bookstores and is a trusted source of books for all businesses and markets. In fact, Amazon KDP uses Ingram to distribute books.

IngramSpark has two big strengths, international shipping and physical presence.

You will be hard pressed to find POD providers with a stronger and larger presence than Ingram. Ingram can help your book get in the right markets if you are looking for overall coverage and availability. Also, since Ingram is based overseas, it is often cheaper to get the book into international markets than domestic ones.

IngramSpark offers soft cover and hardcover binding, along with cream or white paper. Spark really shines through it's option for sizing. They offer more sizing options than others, which makes them ideal if you are very picky about how big the book is.

You will need to provide your own ISBN if you want to go with IngramSpark, they do not provide one for free.

You can see their pricing options here: https://www.ingramspark.com/features

Lulu

http://Lulu.com

Lulu is considered the smallest publishing company of the three, and it is mostly made to help authors get copies of their books.

In general, the author is supposed to be the end-user here, but they do have some distribution options that you might be interested in.

Lulu's biggest strength is that they offer various printing options, and are one of the few to produce hardcover books and multiple binding options (IngramSpark also has hardcover, but Lulu still offers the most binding options and covers). This will be perfect if you want calendars or photo albums. In addition, their various binding options will ensure you get the cover exactly right.

They also offer spiral-bound books as well, which can be the best fit for many low/no content books such as diet journals and recipe books.

They also offer a free ISBN.

Kindle Direct Publishing

https://kdp.amazon.com/

This is Amazon's publishing arm and their exclusive option if you want to go through Amazon specifically.

While you can sell POD books from Lulu on Amazon, you will be charged a fee (which will eat at your profit). You will not be charged if you use KDP.

KDP uses a simple interface so that the publishing process is as easy as possible, which in turn will incredibly reduce the price in most cases.

However, many have noted that the biggest disadvantage is that bookstores will not stock KDP books.

At the same time, having easy and cheap access to Amazon's book market can be worth this disadvantage as bookstore marketing can be exceedingly difficult for first-time authors. Though KDP is used by many different authors, it is best for those who are looking to sell exclusively on Amazon.

KDP offers the least amount of options. You can only do soft cover, and you can choose between a matte or a glossy finish. They also do black or colored printing with cream or white paper.

Pricing

It is standard policy to offer distribution partners a 40-60% discount on books. Some can sell to bookstores, others will not.

See what countries they sell to, how their shipping is, and what their available distribution options are before settling on the distribution model.

If you are also going to ship bulk books to Amazon and sell through their FBA program.

You will also want to check bulk pricing as well. All of three of these options allow you to order books by bulk and resell yourself.

Depending on the niche and type of low/no content book, you can often price these between the $9.99-19.99 range.

5 DESIGNING YOUR BOOK

Now that you have an overview of what printing your book will entail and what company you may want to go with, it is time to look at the actual design of your book.

Here are some programs you can use to create your book.

Microsoft Word

Microsoft Word is a good choice because you can use a variety of done-for-you options.

Sizing templates is possible as mentioned in the printing section of this training.

With the pages that have repetitive content, you can simply select the entire page and copy it as a new page.

Depending on what type of program you use, this can be as simple as selecting all on a page, copying, and pasting.

With Microsoft Word for example, you can even set up a macro to repeat the same action over again.

Want to use Word effectively? Check out my free guide here:

- https://amyharrop.com/pages/publishpermafree/

Using PowerPoint

If you do not want to use Microsoft Word, another way you can easily design and add simple design elements and blank pages to your book is through PowerPoint.

Simply go under your print settings and set the slide specifications to mimic the interior dimensions you have chosen for your book.

Here is a step-by-step guide to the process:

- http://www.goodsgivingback.com/create-ebook-using-powerpoint/

This is a good overview for making sure your PowerPoint book converts to PDF with the proper settings:

- http://www.edteck.com/publish/files/ppt-pub-book2.pdf

InDesign

InDesign is a professional layout program for print from Adobe.

It is what is commonly used to layout magazines and is great for more complicated layouts and for graphics.

While I do not recommend you to dive into it yourself, unless it is something you really want to learn, you can certainly get someone on Fiverr or Odesk to lay out your book in InDesign.

6 BOOK ELEMENTS

Once you have decided on what program to use, you will need to setup and design the sections of your book. You will most likely have these sections:

- The front and back matter of your book
- Any written material
- Artwork
- Layout

Front and Back Matter

If you are using a template, some of the front and back matter will probably be included. You just have to make some changes to make it your own. Depending on the type of book you are doing, you may not need things such as a table of contents or an about the author page. These are not the type of books in which you are branding yourself as an author.

Other Written Material

I recommend adding more value to your low/no content book by having some written material included. You could have an introduction, writing prompts, and exercises or activities section. It does not have to be extensive.

One easy way to include extra value is to have relevant quotes about the subject or topic at hand.

You could put these at the beginning of each page or in the margins. I have provided a spreadsheet with a list of websites that have different quotes which you can use.

For the most part, popular quotes are fine to use as long as they are brief and you credit who said them, if known.

Artwork

The best type of artwork to use with blank books for the interior is vectors.

Vectors have a high resolution and can be scalable, you can insert them into your book as a design element, without having to worry about resolution.

I recommend using simple black and white designs inside your book. That is going to keep the printing cost down.

Here is some more info on vectors and how they are used:

- https://vectr.com/tutorials/what-are-vector-graphics/

Microsoft Word Formats

However, if you are working in Microsoft Word, it can be difficult to insert vectors into your book template.

Microsoft and other companies love their proprietary formats. For example, vectors are often in .ai or .eps format.

For Microsoft Word, you will need to convert them to .emf or .png format and then 'insert as a picture' into your document.

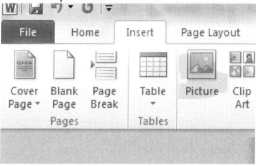

Converting Vector Formats

You can convert your vectors with many free online convertor sites. This is a great task to have an outsourcer do.

Simply collect your images and have them convert them all to .emf or .png.

Here is a good site for all types of file conversions:

- https://cloudconvert.com/

Where to Find Vectors?

There are a number of free vector sites out there which you can download artwork. Just make sure you have commercial use rights.

For some of the sites, all of the vectors are commercial use.

For others, you have to check each individual file. Here are a few sites where you can start your search…

- https://www.freepik.com/

- https://pixabay.com/vectors/search/

- https://www.vector4free.com/free-vectors/Commercial-use

Design Layouts

One of the easiest ways to design the low/no content part of your book is to look for similar design templates and modify them to make them your own.

These are for the sections that are interactive and will usually have tables, columns, and etc.

That does not mean using them as is, as they will normally not be for commercial use, but they will often have the content or organization for the type of book you are creating and you can modify it, change it, or expand on it.

You can:

- Create similar layouts in Word, PowerPoint, or InDesign
- Have a graphic designer create the layouts and give them the samples to model.

Coloring Books

Coloring books are a little different as they do not have a specific layout.

Instead, you will be gathering black and white illustrations. Below are some great resources on creating coloring books.

You can even grab free software to create coloring book images which you can use for your book.

You can get it here:

- http://mycoloringbook.keasoftware.com/

- https://www.instructables.com/id/How-to-Make-a-Coloring-Book/

- http://mycoloringbook.keasoftware.com/create-coloring-pages/81-coloring-pages/113-creating-coloring-pages-with-gimp.html

- https://gomedia.com/zine/tutorials/creating-your-own-coloring-book-using-photoshop/

7 SELLING YOUR LOW OR NO CONTENT BOOK

As I mentioned previously, you should sell your low/no content book two different ways, as a book and as a product.

Selling Low and No Content Books as Books
All three of the recommended print on-demand publishers have extended distribution.

Keep in mind, however, that Lulu and IngramSpark have additional fees, Lulu is $70 while Ingram is $12. And they all have specific requirements for extended distribution.

Selling Books as a Product on Amazon and other Venues
The second way you can sell these books, it is recommended selling them as a traditional book, is

to sell them as a product on primarily Amazon and other venues as well.

The best thing about buying in bulk and having the books fulfilled through Amazon is that you can put the books in various different categories.

Many times, people who are looking for these types of books are not necessarily looking into the books section.

You can dramatically increase your profits by selling these products in the book and other sections.

If you just have the book distributed through a printing partner, then it is treated as a book. That is fine for novels and nonfiction books, but things are different with blank books.

For example, calendars and journals are often considered office or school supplies.

Using Amazon, it allows you to list these books under those categories. Otherwise, the blank books are treated like regular books, which can severely limit your selling potential in this niche since most people who look for blank books are not expecting to find it lumped with novels. This is also perfect for wedding albums and other photo books since Amazon has specific categories for these books.

Fulfillment By Amazon

The specific way you can do this is by using fulfillment by Amazon(FBA).

Amazon's FBA program allows you to send in bulk amounts of your book and then they will fulfill it for you.

They also have the ability to fulfill your book on other platforms such as eBay. So if your book is selling well, you can then put it on other selling platforms.

You will also need to live or be setup as a seller in one of these countries, so it may not be for everyone:

- United States
- Canada
- United Kingdom
- Germany
- France
- Italy
- Japan
- China
- India

Getting Setup With FBA

To send in your books for FBA, you need to go through a number of steps. You need to:

- Register as a Professional Seller
- Order some of your books in bulk-25-100 is a good starter number.
- Create your product listing in one of the product categories
- Get a UPC code for your book
- Send in your books to FBA

Here is an overview of the requirements and the process of their program and also a guide to creating your first shipment to send them:

- http://services.amazon.com/fulfillment-by-amazon/how-it-works.htm

- http://www.onlinesellingexperiment.com/guide-to-creating-your-first-amazon-fba-shipment/

Marketing

These books have a lot of built-in demand, so you do not really need to do massive marketing to start getting sales.

However, there are a few things you should do to set yourself up for success.

- **Title and description**- Spend some time making sure you have a keyword relevant title and compelling description.

  I provided earlier that this training will be a good starting point for you.

  I suggest you look at some of the sample books I have also provided from Amazon, take note of their descriptions and keywords.

  You should model yours on similar books that are already selling.

- **Initial reviews**- As always, it can be good to get some initial reviews so you can build trust on Amazon, which in turn will help you make more sales.
  You can do this by requesting reviews on FB author groups, forums, and your professional or personal network.

- **Importance of category selection**- It is really important to make sure you have your book in the right category.

  You can see look at similar books that are selling in the books category and pick the same category for yours.

  Keep in mind that a specific category may not be available, if you are listing your book through KDP to sell directly on Amazon.

8 CONCLUSION

Low and no content books can be a lucrative area of publishing, because there are endless ways you could appeal to specific demographics.

In addition, this is incredibly easy way to stand out from your competitors and meet an in-demand niche.

Good luck on your publishing journey!

ABOUT THE AUTHOR

Amy Harrop is a writer, product creator, and trainer.

As a Marketer, Author, and Content Publisher, she loves helping people create multiple content income streams.

Her goal is to share what she's learned with anybody who needs help navigating the crowded online marketplace and finding their way in it.

She's created dozens of products, courses, and trainings designed to help you:

- Identify what makes you special
- Create content that communicates your expertise and value
- Amplify your voice so that the people can hear you
- Unlock the profit power of online content

She currently lives in the Northern Idaho area with her husband and two cats. You can learn more at http://amyharrop.com.

Discover the best way to start building your content income stream with the short quiz, **Reveal Your Content Profit Path** here: http://amyharrop.com/quiz.

Get It Here:
https://amyharrop.com/pages/publishpermafree/

Made in the USA
Monee, IL
01 July 2021